JUNETEENTH HANDBOOK

AN EMANCIPATION STORY

More Juneteenth Day Celebration information is available on the Juneteenth Handbook website: sewalott.com.

Copyright Information

First published by Giftkone

© H. Gray 2022

Giftkone Publishing

ISBN: 978-0-9977871-2-2

The quotes in this handbook come from a variety of sources and are assumed to be accurate as quoted in their previous published form, an effort was made to verify each quote source. The publisher cannot guarantee quote perfect accuracy.

TABLE OF CONTENT

FOR MORE INFORMATION CLICK HERE

JTHB

Special Thanks to:

Janice Woodson Moore, Wendy Cochran, Dianne Cathy and Helen Donald for your encouragement and your support.

WHAT IS JUNETEENTH?

The Juneteenth Day celebration is the oldest African American celebration in the United States. A day that marks the first time, slaves in the southern U.S. were publicly informed of the freedom granted to them in President Abraham Lincoln's Emancipation Proclamation; Signaling the collapse of slavery's empire in the U.S.

As news of the end of slavery spread throughout the south, a stunned slave population slowly came to grips with the thought that generations of forced servitude in the United States were over; the celebration that marks the end of slavery in the U.S. is called the Juneteenth Day Celebration. This publication explores the history of some of the people, places, and things associated with the Juneteenth Day celebration and its traditions.

My own personal Juneteenth awakening started back in early 1992 when I was working at Gill Cable, a local cable television company in San Jose California.

Originally hired as a master control room operator my job was to insert local television advertisements, also called commercials, into San Francisco Giant's Baseball games for a sports program titled Giant's Vision.

My production tasks went through many transformations finally landing me in the television director's chair. It was while working as a television director that I first became personally involved with the Juneteenth celebration. Even though both of my parents came from the southern states (Texas, and Louisiana) the first time I ever saw the word Juneteenth was on a flyer advertising the event. Until that time I had no clue what the word Juneteenth meant, then one day, I met two members from the Afro-American Culture Center in San Jose California, Helen Donald, and Brenda Otey. The two women were guests on a local television program I was directing.

In a conversation with them after the interview, I was finally introduced to the true meaning and history behind the oldest African American celebration in this nation.

Expressing an interest in learning more about the Juneteenth celebration I was later asked if I would like to videotape the upcoming Juneteenth Day celebration, organized by the San Jose Afro Center staff. I welcomed the opportunity to learn more about the event and to talk to some of the participants and vendors about their Juneteenth Day experience.

On a sunny slightly breezy day in June 1992, I showed up with my crew of four, composed mostly of family members, and went about preserving the Juneteenth Day event with my video camcorder. Under the partly cloudy sky were all sorts of booths, tents, and displays spread out across the grassy field near the San Jose State University football field. The air was alive with African drum music mixed with the happy sounds of people having a good time. I watched the crowd grow larger as the day went on; my camera lens focusing on vendors selling African clothes from their booth, a mother showing her little daughter the correct way to hold her ice cream cone so that the creamy treat would not fall out of its edible holder.

I captured videotape images of a diverse collection of men, women, and children many dressed in casual street clothes, others dressed in African style garb, all roaming the fairground style environment bargaining with the vendors or laughing it up with family and friends.

Organizations like the Black Fire Fighters, and the Black police officer's, had a booth set up to share information with members of the community they had sworn to protect and serve. There were smiles on their faces as the black police officers and firemen shared information about their chosen profession with interested community members.

Several of the merchants were dressed in African outfits. Seller's tents and booths displayed all sorts of trinkets, clothes, jewelry, even African artworks. The gentle breeze carried past my nose the smell of Barbecue ribs and chicken, popcorn, and warm baked goods all underscored by the sound of African drum music coming from somewhere I could not see. The smell of the good food was really making my videotaping hard to do by then. I was standing videotaping a group of musicians setting up their microphones and electric instruments on a temporarily constructed stage when my hunger pulled me in the direction of food and drink.

The mouthwatering aroma of the food being cooked on the open-air grill and the festive atmosphere was too much for much of my volunteer production crew. Except for my youngest son, Hank Jr., I soon lost the rest of my teenaged team to the Juneteenth Day celebration. Determined, to fight off my urge to eat right then, and to fulfill my promise to capture on videotape as many of the event highlights as I could. I continued my way around to each point of interest pausing just long enough to add another videotaped moment to my growing collection of Juneteenth Day sights and sounds. Finally, content with my harvest of electronically captured videotaped images held securely inside my handheld battery-powered camcorder.

With my backup batteries now in the same shape I was in (in need of recharging) I took a break and followed my nose to some ribs, potato salad, and greens that had been screaming my name for over an hour.

JTHB

The food and a brief rest left me (and my
camera batteries) feeling recharged.

Luckily, I had anticipated the loss of my camera crew, my weekly regiment at the television studio coupled with a job in electronics at Stanford University usually left me ready for some downtime. The Juneteenth Day event in 1991 gave me a chance to spend some up close and personal time with my children while at the same time allowing me to exercise my curiosity about the Juneteenth Day celebration. I came prepared to set up in a spot where I could invite people in front of the camera lens to share their thoughts about the Juneteenth celebration we were attending.

I was looking for anyone willing to pause long enough to say a few words about their Juneteenth experience, and perhaps, comment on the event that had brought so many kinds of people to what many viewed as the oldest end of slavery celebration in America.

After interviewing a few willing participants, I was amazed to learn how little most of the people who stopped to be on camera really knew about the celebration they were attending. Not one of the dozen or more people I spoke with knew the history behind the Juneteenth Celebration. Just before I ended the interview session, I did meet someone who seemed pretty-well versed on the Juneteenth Day event, only to learn as I was packing up my camera gear, that he was in fact, one of the event organizers.

In a way it felt good to know that I was not alone in my lack of understanding about the Juneteenth celebration, but the experience also generated in me a desire to make it a point to inform the people who had suggested I show up with a camera that I felt a great opportunity was being missed to educate the people who came to the event.

Juneteenth means much more than just a festive gathering with good food and drink. My children and I had a great time at the first Juneteenth event we had ever attended. I shared the video information I captured with my camcorder with the San Jose, Afro-Center and wrote a letter to the lady who had invited me and my family. The experience awakened in me the desire to learn more about Juneteenth so I searched my local library and found many scattered bits and pieces about the celebration and wondered what it would be like to take many of the things I had learned and put them together to tell the story of Juneteenth. The results would eventually lead to a screenplay and the creation of my award-winning documentary titled: A time to be remembered; a Juneteenth story. This book gives me a way to include all the information I gathered about the Juneteenth celebration that could not fit into my Juneteenth documentary.

I realize that the words in Abraham Lincoln's Emancipation Proclamation meant not only the end of slaveries territory in the southern U.S. and freedom for thousands of African American people.

Enactment of the document also meant a victory for the abolitionist who had maintained the secret system of boats, tunnels, wagons, and safehouses that made up the Underground Railroad (the UGR). The end of slavery in the U.S. meant that the abolitionist battle against slavery was also over.

Union forces spread throughout the south applying pressure on the retreating rebel armies. As a result, many slaveholders herded their human property (the slaves) further south to the confederate stronghold of Texas. In the state of

Texas, many confederates still clung to the hope that somehow Rebel forces would be victorious in their fight to separate from the union of states and preserve Slaveries Empire in the U.S.

Most, however, were unaware that rather than follow the suggestions from others around him General Robert E. Lee had decided not to divide his confederate forces and participate in a guerrilla war campaign against the north. The general knew that would cost even more north and southern lives. General Robert E. Lee chose to end the bloodshed and surrendered his Virginia army.

Word of Confederate General Robert E. Lee's surrender was followed by the arrival of union General Gordon Granger in Galveston Texas. Upon taking over as governor of that state the general's reading of General Order No.3 put to rest any lingering doubt held by the confederate states about the Civil War's outcome.

The words that would mean the most to the large slave community gathered in Galveston Texas at the time were:
"All slaves are free!"

Former slave owners, sympathetic town's people, and disarmed confederate soldiers could only watch as a joyous outburst combined into a jubilant celebration over the end of the Civil War, and what that meant for African American slaves.

It is doubtful the former slaves heard anything beyond the news that they were finally a free people. The general's suggestion that ex-slaves remain in the homes they were living in and assume the role of a paid laborer went unheeded by many.

Inspite of General Gordon Granger's notification that former slaves would not be allowed to assemble at military posts, hundreds of newly freed African American people would follow the columns of union soldiers north. Some all the way to Washington DC; just to be near father Abraham, the name some former slaves had given to President Abraham Lincoln.

On June 19th, 1865, Abraham Lincoln's words of freedom had finally reached the ears of the last enslaved people from the confederate states. The general's words were final confirmation to the slaves gathered in Galveston Texas that after years of rumor and speculation about their freedom liberation had finally come to them. What had once been whispered amongst the slaves in the field had just been announced publicly for the news reporters, former slave owners, and the general population to hear; the first realization for the slaves that their prayers for freedom had finally been answered.

In the former slaves' vernacular, the joyous news of freedom came to them during (the days between the 13th, and the 19th) the "teenths" of the month and just like the Israelites in Egypt, hundreds of years before them marked their day of deliverance from slavery with the Passover celebration. The newly freed slaves in the southern U.S. chose to remember their day of deliverance from bondage with a special day, and they called that day Juneteenth.

To call Juneteenth solely an African American celebration though does not consider all the contributions made by hundreds of whites, Indians, and other nationalities that kept the safe-houses, wagons, boats, and secret hiding places of the Underground-Railroad system running in the direction of freedom.

The same words of freedom that made thousands of newly liberated slaves raise their voices in cheerful celebration of that moment in time, were also cause for the abolitionist and anti-slavery sympathizers to celebrate.

No longer would the non-black clergy, farmers, shop keepers, or their families need to risk their property, their freedom, or their lives committing the illegal act of helping a runaway slave.

For the abolitionist, their crusade against a system that separated husbands from their wives, parents from their sons and daughters, and showed little regard for human suffering, that same system that sought to retard the mental and spiritual growth of an entire race of individuals based on the color of their skin, was ended.

The abolitionist had successfully maintained the undercover organization, created to help those slaves willing to risk capture, mistreatment, or death, to escape injustice to freedom and in some cases to reunite with family. The U.G.R. offered those brave souls who chose self-emancipation the chance to succeed. To the abolitionist, Juneteenth meant that their contribution and sacrifice in the name of human rights would not go unrewarded.

JUNETEENTH TRADITION

"REFLECTING AND REJOICING FREEING OF THE SLAVES BY CELEBRATING THROUGH DANCING,
EATING, AND CONVERSING WITH FRIENDS AND
RELATIVES." THIS IS WHAT JUNETEENTH MEANS TO ME.

WANDA D. ELLIOTT

While the Juneteenth day observance does not enjoy the status of a national holiday at the time this publication was being written. The event is celebrated nationally in more than thirty states and to-date over 15 different countries.

Presently in Texas, California, the District of Columbia, Michigan, Kentucky, Arkansas, New York, New Jersey, Louisiana, Missouri, Illinois, Connecticut, Alaska, Delaware, Idaho, Iowa, Oklahoma, Florida, and Wyoming, Juneteenth day is recognized as a state holiday. In states like

Arizona, South Dakota, Mississippi, Maryland, Montana, Massachusetts, Colorado, Wisconsin, Pennsylvania, Oregon, and Virginia, the Juneteenth celebration is recognized by either a gubernatorial proclamation or by resolution.

Juneteenth celebrations range from one day to an entire week-long celebration in some places. Traditions include the eating or drinking of something red: red soft- drinks, punch, watermelon, and red velvet cake. The color of red is associated with victory in West African

Society, in the U.S., the color of red at Juneteenth time represents the blood of the African Ancestors, resistance, and strength with plenty of heart.

At some celebrations, the reading of the Emancipation Proclamation is a part of Juneteenth festivities along with horse and wagon parades, marching bands, church choirs, and of course good food (I can bear witness to that). At some Juneteenth celebrations, you will hear drum music and a call to promote reminiscences of family history during, and after, slavery.

The state of Texas boasts the largest, week-long, Juneteenth celebration in the nation. The state's first Juneteenth celebration was set in motion by the Freedmen's Bureau, the organization set up in 1867 to assist the newly freed slaves. Five years later the Juneteenth celebration earned a place on the calendar of public events in Texas; once upon a time attracting as many as thirty-thousand African Americans to a place called Comanche Crossing, also known as

JTHB

Booker T. Washington Park, in Limestone
County Texas.

During the racially charged, Civil Rights, period of the 1960s in the south, many Juneteenth celebrations went on the decline. As more people from the southern states moved to other areas around the country and served in the U.S. military around the world, the importance of the Juneteenth celebration and the meaning and importance of its traditions began to be recognized by different community-based organizations, at home in the U.S. and as far away as Germany; people began to explore and understand what an important part of African American History the Juneteenth Day Celebration is. Since then, the understanding and importance of the oldest African American celebration in the country have been on the rise.

In the little town of Allensworth California, situated halfway between San Francisco and Los Angeles, busloads of people are treated to the largest Juneteenth celebration in the state of California; the event features Blues festivals, pageants, dramatic readings, even baseball games have become part of the Juneteenth Day Celebration.

JTHB

THE HISTORY OF JUNETEENTH

THE "N" WORD

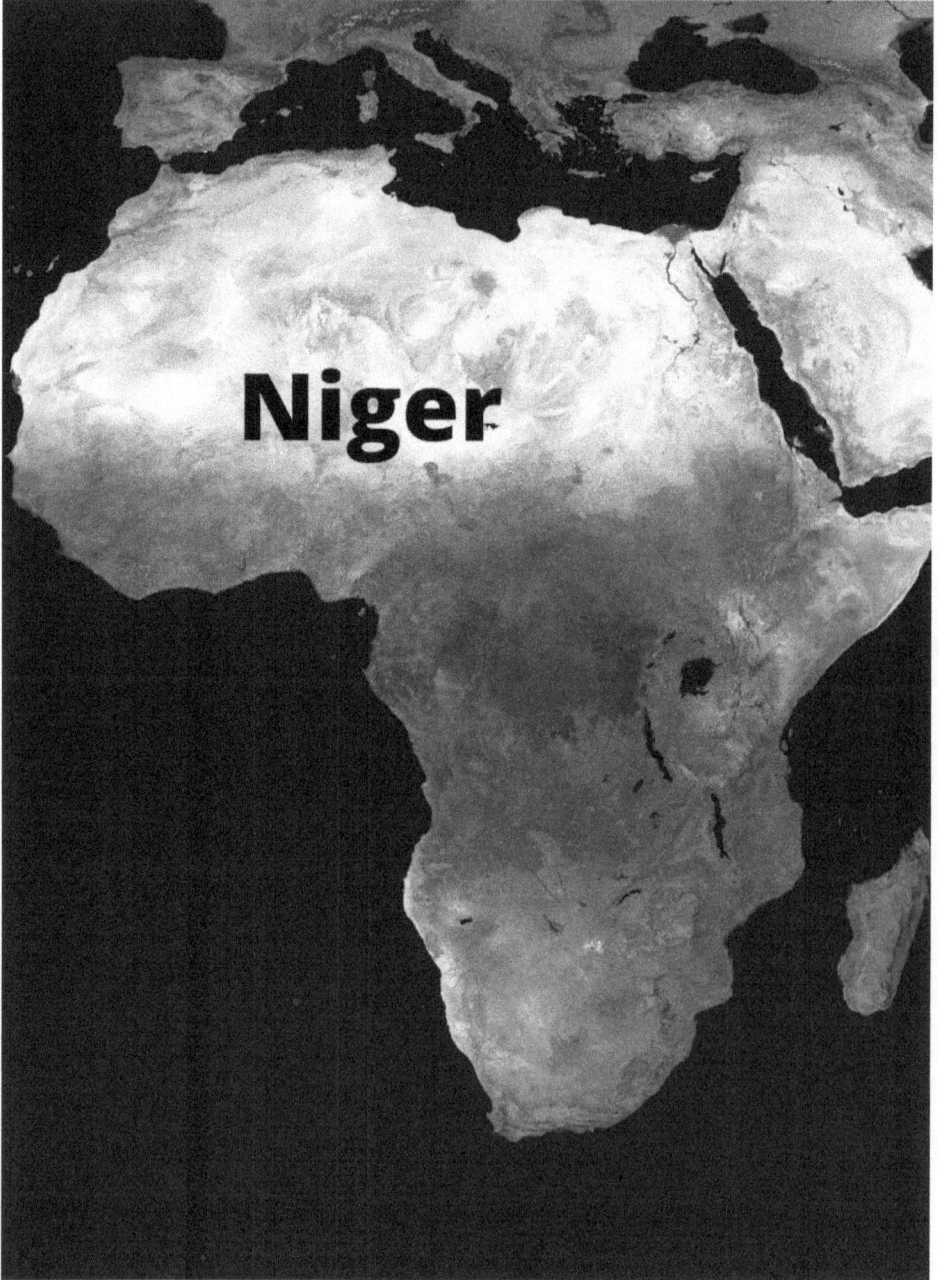

"Niger" (pronounced Ni-jeer) can be found in the west-central part of the African continent. The African states of Niger and Nigeria took their names from the Niger River. It is the third longest river in Africa surpassed in length only by the Nile and the Congo Rivers. The River Niger's boomerang shape spreads itself over more than four thousand two hundred kilometers (or 2,600 miles) of the West Africa landscape. From the over two hundred miles long bend in the river that travels past the fabled city of Timbuctoo, the Niger River also flows southwest into Guinea and Sierra Leone; southeast to Niger through Nigeria all the way to the South Atlantic Ocean.

The mysterious ribbon of relatively clear water is thought to be the product of two mighty rivers that long-ago converged to produce the Niger River of today. How the river got its name is a mystery anthropologist may uncover one day, but to-date none of the thirty languages spoken in the Niger River delta or its river basin has shown conclusive proof of the name's origin.

While the name Nigeria was a European imperialist creation suggested in 1890 by the British journalist, Flora Shaw, some believe the Niger River's name came from the indigenous people. It is doubtful that the waterway's name came from the Portuguese who were among the first to explore Africa. The Niger River is not a Rio Negro (black-water-river) Negro, is the Latin word for black. From near the legendary city of Timbuktu, located along the Niger River, there is a Tuareg phrase, gheren, which translated means: the river of rivers. Over time "gheren" was shortened to "ngher." The River Niger was known to the Romans who referred to the African inland waterway as, Dasibari.

The Songhay people called the Niger-River, Isa Ber, (meaning big river) Joliba (Great River) was the word the Mandigo people used to describe the river Niger. The Niger River is the most nearby major water source to the Saharan desert, and deserves the name of life-giver, because from the Bozo fishermen who cast their fishing nets into the river's translucent waters, the Fulani cattle herdsmen who water their thirsty livestock at the water's edge, to the hundreds of tiny villages that dot the

JTHB

Niger River shoreline, the Niger river is a source of life.

For hundreds of years, the banks of the Niger River were also a source of slaves, the Bozo and Balla ethnic groups along with the Fulani and Songhay were all once slaves of the Tuareg.

NIGERIA THE MOTHERLAND

Long before slavery immigrated to North America it was widespread in Nigeria. Each of the major groups, the Hausa in the north the Lgbo in the east, and the Yoruba in the west used slave labor.

Driven by a quest for riches and glory the first Portuguese slave ships to Africa arrived with slaves to sell. They traded their captive cargo for the gold that was obtainable on Africa's gold coast.

When the new American colonies sought slave labor the Portuguese were quick to profit from the growing colonial need for slave labor. Making Portugal's enduring legacy to Nigeria the initiation of the transatlantic slave trade, and the eventual forced migration of more than three million people between the years of 1650 and 1860 to the American colonies that grew into a union of states.

Near the end of the sixteenth century, the Dutch navy challenged Portugal and put an end to the monopoly held until then by the Portuguese transatlantic slave trade. The Dutch took over all the Portuguese trading stations along the African west coast and diverted the flow of slave sales money away from the Portuguese to the Dutch.

Drawn by the lucrative profits in human cargo the French and British would compete for a place in the slave trade economy and eventually undermine the Dutch slave trading stronghold. In the years that followed ships flying the flags of France, Sweden, Denmark, and several other European maritime countries would join in the legal trafficking of African slaves across the Atlantic Ocean to the American colonies.

A revolution in France would bring the French participation in the slave trade to an end and by the eighteenth century, Great Britain would stand alone as the dominant transatlantic slave trading power in the world.

THE TRADE TRIANGLE

Loaded with goods to trade for the slaves, British ship sailed the first leg of the trade triangle from England to the west coast of Africa smelling of damp hemp ropes, canvas, and the sea. In Africa, the trade cargo was taken ashore and the human cargo: African men, women, and children, were loaded onboard a waiting ship and jam-packed by the hundreds below deck. Chained together in the tight confines of the ship's hold the mortality rate amongst the captives sometimes ran higher than 30 percent.

To compensate for the high losses, it was common for slaves to be overcrowded into the ship's hold. From Africa, the ship headed west across the Atlantic Ocean toward America on the second leg of the trade triangle voyage, also known as the middle passage. It was during the middle passage that the ship took on the stench of human suffering; odors of sea sickness, dysentery, burned flesh, and death permeated the cramped inhumane space where the slaves were confined. Many slaves had fresh unhealed flesh burns from the hot branding irons used to mark women's breast, the backs, and arms of men and boys. Some of the sailors serving on a British slave ship were there as a form of punishment, for crimes against the British navy, and because of their misfortune could be particularly cruel to slave captives adding another layer of misery to an uncertain plight.

Dead slaves along with those who were too sick, or those thought to be contagious, were taken up on deck and unceremoniously tossed over the side to a watery grave that would not tolerate any tombstone, or any other marker of remembrance except for perhaps a note in the ship's log denoting a loss of revenue.

Upon arrival in America, the slaves were offloaded into holding pens. The ship was washed cleaned, and in exchange for its human payload, reloaded with sugar, cotton, and tobacco. The British vessel laden with American goods was then free to return to England completing the third and final leg of its journey around the trade triangle. The odors of pain and suffering soaked up by the shadowy confines of the ship's hold replaced by the sweet smell of success from another profitable voyage around the slave trade triangle.

Every part of Nigeria was affected by the slave trade making it a slave trading hub. Slaves were sent in two directions, across the Sahara Desert, and to the African west coast. In the eighteenth century, more slaves came from the Nigerian coast than from the African region of Angola.

Angola supplied more than forty percent of all African slaves shipped to America during the transatlantic trade. The African state of Benin had virtually isolated itself from transatlantic slave trade with an embargo on the export of slaves. Benin continued to employ captured slaves in its domestic economy, however, the Edo state refused to participate in the transatlantic exportation of African people.

JTHB

"MY MEMORY IS NEARLY GONE NOW, BUT I CAN REMEMBER TWO THINGS, THAT I AM A GREAT SINNER, AND THAT CHRIST IS A GREAT SAVIOR"

JOHN NEWTON

Slave ship captain John Newton was eighty-two-years-old when he spoke those words. He had gone through many transformations before he reached that reflective age.

Starting with the death of his mother, when he was eight years old, his father, a demanding merchant ship captain, removed young John Newton from the divinity school he had been left at and took his son to live onboard his sailing ship. By the time John Newton was eleven years old his father had transformed him into a gifted sailor. On the deck of a British merchant ship sailing the Mediterranean Sea was where John Newton grew into a young man. His next transformation came at the age of eighteen when he found himself a regimented, spit-and-polish, crewman on a proud British man-of-war, a Royal Navy warship where military regiment and tradition reigned supreme.

Forced to enlist in the British Navy, a young adult John Newton, resisted the notion of trading his individuality for the joint effort called for by the Royal Navy. He missed the loosely regimented routine onboard the merchant ship. The British Navy ran its ships with an iron hand from the groomed sailor's uniform to the pomp and ceremony of the British Royal Navy.

Rebellious and unable to make the adjustment to the military way of life John Newton deserted both his ship and the British Navy.

Later when he was captured by the British John Newton found himself on yet another British vessel, only this ship did not possess the fine trim and armament of the full of pride British man-of-war. For his crime of desertion, John Newton was sent to serve onboard a British slave-ship. As he toiled in disgraced servitude, day in and day out, John Newton was witness to the mistreatment of those whose only crime was having dark skin. Even though his skin color was not the color the British were buying or selling he knew what it felt like to be forced away from home and made to work hard without pay. He knew what it was like to be poorly clothed, badly fed, and mistreated by those thinking themselves more superior. When his service aboard the British slave ship was done John Newton was discharged from the Navy and marooned on the west coast of Africa.

The abandoned British sailor was able to find employment with a slave trader, however, he was distrusted, and disliked, by the slave merchant's African wife and soon found himself working, living, and eating with the slaves. A member of the British ship Greyhound's crew spotted the British subject working alongside the slaves and in an act of mercy returned John Newton to England. During that voyage home, John Newton found the book that would spark yet another transformation in his life.

The book was called Imitation of Christ, by Thomas A. Kempis. As John Newton tolerated the long shipboard hours, he thought about the brutal conditions imposed upon him because he sought the freedom he had been born with, he took from the book the seed of Christianity and it began to renovate his soul.

Maturity stilled the uncertainty of his youth and John grew both as a sailor and a Christian. It was not long before his life's experiences helped him get promoted to the rank of ship's master. It was during his days as a slave ship captain sailing the Atlantic that his new-found Christian beliefs often clashed with the act of slavery that was now his livelihood.

The slave trade was acceptable in England in the middle 1700s; slave commerce filled the British need for American goods like Tobacco and cotton. Deeply troubled by the inhumane aspect of the slave trade John Newton found himself at an impasse that would result in his decision to leave the sea, the environment he had grown up in, and the place that had been his home for most of his life.

Attitudes about the slave trade were more than three-hundred years slow in changing but the British would eventually outlaw the trading of people as slaves in 1807; going so far as to set up blockades along the African coast to enforce their controversial new policy.

In 1808, more than fifty years before the Civil War, an act of the U.S. Congress would make it illegal to continue to import slaves from outside of the country and American navy ships would join British navy ships to strengthen the blockade against the transatlantic slave trade.

Some, but not all, of the illegal import of slaves from Africa was halted by the joint cooperative actions of America and Great Britain, reducing the flow of people commonly referred to by slave ship captains as black gold, and preventing the taking of African people out of Africa.

However, driven by merchants and slave owners in America it would be the American merchant ship captains that became good at evading the British and American blockade, continuing to deliver their smuggled slaves, illegally, to the U.S.

For the blockade running captains, the added risk meant they could demand more money from the farmers and merchants who paid them. Over time the blockade would begin to have the desired effect and while the money offered to them for defying British and American law never really dried up fewer and fewer ship's captains wanted to risk losing everything they had worked for or spending time in prison.

Add to that the changing political climate, runaway slaves, the threat of a slave revolt, along with a growing

abolitionist movement in America and a
perfect storm of opposition to slavery
set in motion the chain of events that
would eventually lead to the Civil War.

SELF EMANCIPATION

NEWSPAPER ADS FROM THE 1800's

"$500.00 reward for a runaway slave; ran away on Saturday, the 23rd instant, before 12 O'clock from the subscriber, residing in Rockville Montgomery County, My Negro girl Ann Maria Weenis, about 15 years of age; a bright mulatto; some small freckles on her face; slender in person, thick suit of hair inclined to be sandy. Her parents are free and reside in Washington DC. She was taken away by someone in a carriage, probably by a white man, by whom she may be carried beyond the limits of the state of Maryland."

"Absconded from the Forest-Plantation of the late Dunbar, on Sunday the 7th instant, a very handsome Mulattress called Harriet, about 13 years of age, with straight dark hair and dark eyes. The girl was lately in New Orleans and is known to have seen there a man who she claims is her father, and who does now or did lately live on the

Mississippi, a little above the mouth of the Chafalaya. It is highly probable some plan has been concerted for the girls escape."

"$200.00 reward; run away on Saturday night the 5th instant July 1856 from the subscriber, Ned Brannun, a slave 28 years of age about 5 foot 8 inches high, bright mulatto, a thick suit of straight black hair, very little beard, gray eyes, and light-colored eyebrows. He is quietly intelligent and has a find address. He is well acquainted in Washington City, DC and is doubtless aided by abolitionist influenced to reach a free state most likely in a vessel freighted with coal from Georgetown."

"$300.00 Reward; ran away from the subscriber from the neighborhood of Town Point, on Saturday night the 24th inst., my Negro man Aaron Cornish, about 35 years old. He is about five feet ten inches high, black, good looking, rather pleasant countenance, and carries himself with a confident manner. He went off with his wife, Daffney, a Negro woman belonging to Renben E. Phillips. I will give the above reward if taken out of the county, and $200.00 if taken in the

county: in either case to be lodged in Cambridge Jail."

"$300.00 reward, Ran away from the subscriber, on Saturday night last, 17th inst., my Negro woman Lizzie, about 28 years old. She is medium sized, dark complexion, good-looking. She was well dressed, wearing a red and green blanket Shaw, and carried her a variety of clothing. She ran off in the company with her husband, Nat Amby, belonging to John Uri Esq., who is about 6 feet in height, with slight impediment in his speech, dark chestnut color, and large scar on the side of his neck."

"Ran away $500.00 reward; Left the tobacco factory of the subscriber, on the 14th inst., on the pretense of being sick, a mulatto man, named Elijah, the property of Maj. Edward Johnson, of Chesterfield County. He is about 5 feet 8 or 10 inches high, spare made, bushy hair, and very genteel appearance; he is supposed to be making his way north. The above reward will be paid if delivered at the factory."

Long before the first mention of the underground-railroad newspapers in the early eighteen-hundreds were dotted with newspaper ads like the ones above. Slaves had been self-emancipating themselves for years. Some worked and saved to purchase their own freedom or the freedom of a family member. In some cases, where a slave owner had children by a slave woman, provisions were made through a Deed of Manumission, or a will, for their children to be freed once the child reached a certain age. Others simply claimed whatever opportunity came their way and ran away.

Freed slaves did little better than their enslaved counterpart in many areas. Some places in the south required that a free colored person choose a master if they wanted to live in that state. In the north, some African Americans became successful business owners by educating themselves but even the most successful former slaves could have their freedom ripped away from them by unscrupulous kidnappers dealing in the underground slave trade.

In a nation divided against itself when it came to the slavery question, many legal loopholes existed to protect those who wished to protect or profit from the institution of slavery. What little legislation there was for the slave seemed better suited to protect them as chattel, not people; for the unfortunate, colored individuals who fell victim to the kidnappers or slave catchers, there was little that could be done to help them remain free. The laws at that time provided more protection for the kidnappers and slave catchers than it did for their victims, the slaves.

For the slave that chose to self-emancipate, her or himself the road ahead was filled with risks and uncertainty. Runaway slaves usually suffered at the hands of merciless overseers determined to make an example of any runaway slave. The mistreatment was usually handed out with approval from the slave owner. The runaway slave was often put on display so that other slaves could see the high price to be paid for choosing to run away, and as a reminder that the slave-hunters would be on their trail the moment they went missing, the punishment was usually severe. For the runaway slave that got caught; torture, dismemberment, or being hobbled, (made to permanently walk with difficulty) were all methods used to punish a runaway slave.

JTHB

RIDING ON THE UNDERGROUND RAILROAD

The metaphor for the secret system of safe houses hidden passageways and trails that helped runaway slaves avoid capture was the Underground Railroad. It might sound hard to believe but the first underground railroad did not run in the direction of freedom. After the importation of slaves from the west coast of Africa was banned by congress in 1808 slavery owners, and merchants started their own version of the underground railroad and broke the law too. They set up their own safe houses, covert transportation, and overseer conductors all working together to deliver their illegal cargo of African slaves to the south and into slavery.

For the underground railroad that ran in the direction of freedom its conductors, engineers, and station keepers were the abolitionist, and its passenger's fugitive slaves in search of freedom from slavery.

The supporters of slavery, the slaveholders used slaves as a labor force, for the slave merchants, slaves were a source of income and tradeable property. Those who benefited from the slave trade wanted to see the U.G.R derailed and disassembled. The slaveholders and merchants viewed the abolitionist who maintained the U.G.R. system as a well-organized ring of thieves determined to set free their legal property.

Protests, against slavery began with the introduction of slavery in the Colonies and continued until the end of the Civil War in 1865. Over the years the abolitionist movement, made up of anti-slavery advocates from every nationality in the colonies grew into a force that enraged slaveholders.

Abolitionist like Oberlin Colleges' Owen Brown, whose family history could be traced back to the Pilgrim ship the Mayflower, chose a relatively passive method of opposing slavery by maintaining a station on the U.G.R. His son, John chose violence to combat the indifference and racism of slavery.

Driven by confrontation and his own sense of justice, John Brown gave his life, and the lives of two of his sons, in a failed robbery attempt of a U.S. armory at Harper's Ferry Virginia. John Brown's plan was to arm slaves in the south and lead them in an armed uprising against the slave owners.

The majority, of abolitionists found other more none-violent ways of resistance to the slavery system. The underground railroad was one of the least violent means of secret resistance, however, the risk from such a choice was considerable. Helping a runaway slave was against the law. To be caught assisting a fugitive slave could mean the loss of your property, time in jail, even death.

Still, hundreds of people, black, white, Native American, and others looked past the differences of skin color and saw unfair laws that did not live up to the words in our constitution and did not treat all men and women equally. Working together the abolitionist mounted a campaign to amend the laws of the nation. The diversity of those who worked on the U.G.R. would prove to be one of the greatest strengths of the abolitionist when dealing with those who wanted to

JTHB

divide the country into only two colors
one black and one white.

SELF-EMANCIPATED ABOLITIONIST

FREDERICK DOUGLAS

In February 1818, Miss Harriet Bailey, a Negro slave, gave birth to a son she named Fredrick Augustus Washington Bailey. His father was a white slave owner. Young Fredrick possessed the heart and mind of a free man and at an early age, he saw the slave conditions he lived in with his mother as unacceptable. Several failed attempts to escape his life of bondage did not detour young Frederick Bailey from trying to gain his freedom. Finally, one day his determination paid off when he succeeded in self-emancipating himself.

At the end of his journey, he would find himself alone in New York City. Bailey knew from his other failed attempts to run from slavery that people would be looking for him. Watching slave catchers, aided by both black and white informants close in on and capture runaway slaves on the streets of New York City young Bailey soon realized that placing his trust in the wrong person could lead to a long distasteful return trip down south; in the clutches of an unsympathetic slave catcher. Being observant, and cautious,

Fredrick Bailey chanced upon an agent of the Underground Railroad and his self-renovation began.

It was suggested by his friend, Nathan Johnson, that Fredrick Bailey choose another name to throw off the ever-present slave hunters and their undercover agents. Selecting the name, Douglas, from the book he was reading at the time, titled Lady of the Lake, Fredrick Bailey became Fredrick Douglas.

He would go on to become a prominent and outspoken African American voice for the abolition of slavery and the fight against discrimination in the United States.

"I HATED SLAVERY ALWAYS, AND MY DESIRE FOR FREEDOM NEEDED ONLY A FAVORABLE BREEZE TO FAN IT TO A BLAZE AT ANY MOMENT. THE THOUGHT OF BEING A CREATURE OF THE PRESENT AND THE PAST TROUBLED ME, AND I LONGED TO HAVE A FUTURE, A FUTURE WITH HOPE IN IT."

FREDERICK DOUGLASS

His life of prominence would not be without its problems. Speaking under his assumed name the specter of his past followed him everywhere he went. There was always the worry that his real identity would be discovered sending him back into a life of servitude.

Two British friends of Frederick Douglas, who were aware of his concern, raised the required amount of $710.95 and sent it to Hugh Auld the man who held the title for Douglas and on December 5, 1846, Hugh Auld put his name on the paper that would make the 28-year-old Frederick Douglas a free man.

Many in the abolitionist community would not be happy with that turn of events, among them Frederick Douglas himself. While he appreciated the gesture, to Douglas, Hugh Auld was his kidnapper not his master and the money collected and paid for his freedom merely a ransom.

Douglas would later be criticized by fellow abolitionist for allowing his freedom to be purchased, and he would draw criticism again from followers for marrying a white woman while championing the black cause.

After his first wife, Anna Murray, a black woman died, Douglas would find himself scorned by the children from his first marriage and some of his followers for marrying his secretary, Helen Pitt; a white woman to whom he was twenty years her senior.

"IT BOTHERS ME NOT THAT THERE SEEMS NO END TO OTHERS CONCERN WITH MY AFFAIRS.

HOW CAN I CHAMPION A CAUSE WHEN I AM DIVIDED IN MY RACIAL LOYALTY SOME HAVE SAID?

WHY DO I DISHONOR MY AFRICAN ROOTS?

BY TAKING A WHITE WIFE? TO WIT I ANSWER MY FIRST WIFE HONORED MY MOTHER'S RACE, AND MY SECOND WIFE MY FATHERS".

FREDERICK DOUGLASS

HARRIET TUBMAN

Harriet Tubman would be given the name the black Moses for guiding so many runaway slaves to freedom. She was born Araminta Ross in 1821. Her parents Harriet Greene, and Benjamin Ross, were both slaves on a large plantation in Dorchester County Maryland. She grew up in a one-room shack with no windows. When Harriet was only six years old, she was removed from her family and put to work on a neighboring plantation as a house slave. Little Harriet would be hired away from her family three times before she was ten years old.

During the time away from her mother and father, Harriet developed bronchitis and suffered through the measles. On her back were scarring from the frequent whipping she had received for showing the defiance that would eventually make her a legend. By the time Harriet was allowed to work in the field more than half of her young life had been spent toiling long and hard in the homes of different masters. The bronchitis she endured would leave

Harriet with the deep husky voice that those close to her would come to recognize. Work in the field was more demanding than the household tasks she was used to but the change in work environments gave a youthful Harriet Ross the chance to hear stories told by the other slaves working alongside her.

Harriet listened to the stories being told by those around her; tales about colored men and women who had followed the north star to freedom.

One day Harriet angered an overseer who was in the process of disciplining another slave caught trying to run away. When she refused to bind the man's hands as she was told the angry overseer came down hard across Harriet's head with a heavy metal bar. Knocked unconscious; her skull fractured she lie near death for weeks before regaining consciousness. It would take a long time for Harriet to get back on her feet, but she was eventually well enough to leave her sickbed. She would never fully recover from that brutal attack and for the rest of her life she would be plagued by frequent headaches, dizzy spells, and blackouts.

Neither the attack nor its consequence would weaken Harriet's determination to resist the way she and the other slaves were treated. Recalling the stories told by the slaves in the field and paying close attention to the reasons so many slaves got caught she vowed not to make the same mistakes. The day would come when Harriet was able to self-emancipate herself and when she did, she did not forget about the many family members and friends she left behind. With her determination and will, she would obtain the freedom she desired, and over the years Harriet Ross would marry a man named John Tubman and assume the name most history books know her by, she would go on to risk the freedom she had earned for herself by traveling back into areas where there was a price on her head, to lead those, brave enough to accompany her to freedom.

"A MORE ORDINARY SPECIMEN OF HUMANITY COULD HARDLY BE FOUND AMONG THE MOST

UNFORTUNATE-LOOKING FARM HANDS OF THE

SOUTH YET, IN POINT OF COURAGE,

SHREWDNESS, AND DISINTERESTED EXTERIOR

TO RESCUE HER FELLOW-MEN, BY MAKING PERSONAL VISITS TO MARYLAND AMONG THE

SLAVES, SHE WAS WITHOUT HER EQUAL."

WILLIAM STILL

Most of the time Harriet Tubman gave the appearance of being asleep on her feet, but inside her head churned the mind of a fox. While she often exhibited a disregard for her own life, traveling where there was a price on her head, she was both careful and watchful were those she was piloting were concerned. Harriet Tubman was a truly self-emancipated abolitionist. While those around her pondered and discussed how to end slavery. Harriet Tubman took it upon herself to free her people, one person at a time if she had to.

WILLIAM STILL

Born, October 7, 1821, William Still was the youngest of eighteen children. He would grow up to be a successful businessman, a loving husband devoted father, and a conductor on the clandestine organization called the underground railroad. The son of former slaves, Levin and Charity Still, William's wit and his ability to work hard would take him from the rags he grew up in on the farm to the riches he amassed as a prominent and successful coal business owner in Philadelphia. He became a tireless worker on the Philadelphia underground railroad and as a result, a coincidental meeting on a Philadelphia Street with a man he suspected of being a runaway slave would turn into a life-changing experience for William Still; an experience that would forever strengthen his resolve to reunite African American families separated by slavery. William approached the out of place looking man on the street and befriended him. The man told him that he went by the name of Peter. In the conversation that followed, William Still was not at all surprised to learn that Peter was a runaway slave, however, William found himself completely flabbergasted to learn that the man he was trying to help was, in fact, his own brother, Peter Still.

Peter and some of their other siblings had been left behind by their mother, Charity, when she ran away to be with her husband Levin. Levin Still had managed to purchase his own freedom but could not afford to free his wife and several of their eighteen children who had remained behind with their mother.

Struck by the realization that there were many other slave families, just like his own, scattered by the anti-African American family institution of slavery William Still was determined to acquire as much information about those he assisted on the U.G.R., as possible. Hoping that one day the information he gathered might help in reuniting families separated by slavery. His idea for the Vigilance Committee, an organization meant to walk the streets of Philadelphia on the lookout for runaway slaves, was the result of that chance meeting with a runaway slave, who turned out to be William Still's own brother.

Almost ten years after the Civil War ended, William Still gathered together the journal he kept secretly hidden and in 1872 he published the written accounts of his involvement with the people and places connected to the U.G.R., William Still's rare and well-kept time stamped accounts of routine U.G.R. operations, titled The Underground Railroad, tells of the money he distributed to Harriet Tubman, John Brown, and to other abolitionists who often took themselves into harm's way to assist slaves on the run.

The interviews that William Still conducted with newly arrived fugitive slaves all became part of the written record he maintained. Unlike several of the other abolitionist accounts that tended to paint runaway slaves as helpless passengers on the U.G.R. William still's writings decorated runaway slaves as the heroes and heroines they were.

Philadelphia was the Grand Central Station of the U.G.R.; a centralized hub where abolitionist conductors and engineers sheltered and helped transport runaway slaves on their journey to the promise land. Reunited by chance with his own family member, his brother Peter, William Still's work to chronicle the comings and goings of hundreds of different slaves; and he helped many of the slaves who came his way to rejoin their family.

Abolitionist, Thomas Garret wrote, "December 29th, Wilmington; Esteemed Friend, J. Miller Mc Kim: We made arrangement last night and sent away Harriet Tubman, with six men and one woman to Allen Agnew's, to be forwarded across the county to the city. Harriet and one of the men had worn their shoes off their feet, and I gave them two

JTHB

dollars to help fit them out, but do not
yet know the expense."

Thomas Garrett

Born August 21st, 1789, a Quaker from birth, Thomas Garrett, would first take up the antislavery cause at the age of twenty-five. From that point until his death, at the age of eighty-one, Thomas Garrett would not fail to assist any fugitive from slavery that came his way.

In the pro-slavery community around him, Garrett's antislavery stand had cost him most of his friendships, put him under almost constant police surveillance, and in nearby Maryland, authorities offered a reward for his arrest.

His written account of his involvement with the U.G.R. would show that he had assisted more than twenty-one hundred slaves in their bid for freedom, and that number did not include the many fugitives Thomas Garrett had helped before his work on the Underground-Railroad.

Garrett's strong religious beliefs drove his opposition to slavery and steered him to join the Pennsylvania Abolition Society. His house became a station on the U.G.R. usually the last stop for runaway slaves who made it that far. Garrett did little to hide the fact that he was committed to helping runaway slaves reach freedom, and made it clear to those around him that he planned to continue his work as a station keeper on the U.G.R.

As a result, he was forced into bankruptcy from the heavy fines imposed on him by the federal court. When it came to his belief that slavery was wrong Thomas Garrett did not back down. The courage of his convictions would win Garret new supporters, many of them African American. During the Civil War, African Americans formed volunteer groups to watch over Garrett's family and property and protect their brave and outspoken antislavery voice against any pro-slavery retaliation.

Understanding and forthright Thomas Garrett was a true hero and a devoutly religious man that truly-believed all men were created equal. His beliefs allowed him to operate without fear and his supporters would eventually help him re-establish his business in the iron trade.

After the Civil War began Thomas Garrett remarked regarding slavery, that "the nation went into business by the wholesale, so I quit my retail operations."

What I believe he meant by that was that with the end of the Civil War and the government now supporting the abolishment of slavery there was no need for an underground railroad or any of its supporters.

Garrett was carried through the streets of Wilmington Delaware on a wagon driven by joyous African Americans after the passage of the 15th Amendment was announced. That amendment gave African American men the right to vote. On each side of the wagon, surrounded by a moving mass of smiling colored faces, were painted the words "Our Moses."

TWO UNDERGROUND RAILROADS

Slave owners and merchants viewed the hidden railroad operation as organized theft committed by a well-organized gang of determined abolitionist. This is a view that is somewhat ironic in my opinion since there is some evidence that the first underground railroad was run by slave owners and merchants themselves. My research showed that slave owners and merchants had created their own secret system of concealed hideouts, and hidden pathways that did not run in the direction of freedom. An underground railroad that operated with the expressed purpose of continuing to bring African people into slavery illegally.

The slave trade from abroad was banned by the U.S. congress in 1808 but American slave merchants and slave owners secretly developed a way to keep a flow of new slaves coming to America from Africa. A secretive process that went on despite a U.S. and British blockade set up off the west coast of Africa to prevent slaves from being brought to the U.S.

On the devils-underground railroad, the route went from the north to the south. There was an organized network of kidnappers and slave transporters, not the abolitionist. The merchants and slave owners had set up a system of safe houses to hide and rest the slave smugglers, and their victims.

A couple of names associated with the bad underground railroad were John Crenshaw and Patty Cannon. More than once Crenshaw had been indicted for the crime of kidnapping free African Americans, transporting them south and selling them into slavery. Free African American people, ignorant of Crenshaw's operation, were tricked into thinking they were receiving a free flatboat voyage down river only to find out too late that it was a deception that had cost them their freedom.

One of the most notorious of these kidnappers was Patty Cannon. Her villainous career became the stuff that ghostly tales are made from.

In 1826, Patty Cannon worked on what I call the anti-version of the Underground Railroad and for the poor unfortunate souls who wandered Patty's way, lured by her gang's promise of freedom, the road often led to torture and death. The kidnapped victims who survived usually found themselves on an underground railroad to hell; and headed away from the promise land. Patty Cannon was a tall woman with striking features. Her trademark was her rough language and demeanor. A merciless slave hunter, Patty along with her husband, Joe Johnson, ran a slave trading business. A large woman with a mean streak to match, Patty Cannon was said to be able to throw a man to the ground by his hair. She and her gang captured fugitive slaves and kidnapped free colored American people.

Sussex County near the Nanticoke River was where Patty Cannon and her gang operated. Located at the corner of Dorchester County and Carolina County in Maryland, Patty, and her gang, made up of whites and a few renegade blacks were in the business of fooling fugitives and free colored Americans into what appeared to be a safe place before springing their trap. To evade capture by the police Patty and her gang would escape across the Delaware state line conveniently located just across from Maryland.

Local lawmen were determined to put Patty Cannon and her gang of kidnappers out of business when it became known that some of the victims, she and her band of outlaws had tortured and killed were children.

Patty Cannon's deceitful career came to an end when she was finally captured in a joint law enforcement effort that had anticipated her use of the nearby Delaware border to escape. She was held for trial after she confessed to the murder of four fugitive slaves, two of them children. On May 11, 1829, an outraged public waited outside Patty Cannon's George Town Delaware jail cell eager to witness her execution; but Patty Cannon had one last trick up her sleeve. Guards would find Patty Cannon dead in her jail cell. She had poisoned herself cheating the angry mob out of their anticipated spectacle. Her husband Joe Johnson was sentenced to and received 39 lashes.

Behind the bar at the Water View Hotel there was an opening that led to the Nanticoke River where a small island used to be. Patty Cannon and her gang used that tunnel to transport kidnapped victims to waiting boats for a voyage into bondage on the devil's underground railroad. Her death ended her reign of terror in the area, however, her legend lived on to terrify several generations of young children living in the Delaware region where Patty and her gang carried on their fiendish business. For years after Patty Cannon's demise all a parent had to do to quiet an overactive child was to say: "Patty Cannon's going to get you."

THE UNDERGROUND RAILROAD TO FREEDOM

The Underground Railroad that ran in the direction of freedom is the underground railroad most people are familiar with. The stations along the U.G.R. that ran toward the promise lands were safe havens with secret rooms, crawl spaces, and underground hiding places to shelter fugitive slaves and provide them with food, drink, and a place to rest.

Hidden away from the slave hunters who were in many cases supported by the authorities, runaway slaves were given an infusion of hope.

While Africans, and African Americans, suffered the indignation of slavery, and the mental and physical anguish associated with a life of bondage, they were not alone in their prayer to end slavery. Thousands of white people in the north and in the south, farmers and statesmen protested the institution of slavery by helping runaway slaves in their quests to live as a free person.

For the non-African American souls that supported the U.G.R. system, they also risk losing their property, their freedom, and their life, if they were caught. People like Harriett Tubman, William Still, are the famous black abolitionist, but there were many different races of people working on the U.G.R. that made up a diverse group of engineers, conductors, and station keepers, whose clandestine work on the U.G.R. kept the secret system on track and running until the U.G.R. was no longer necessary. The Abolitionist were former slaves, white reformers, and clergy, who accepted the risks associated with helping set free hundreds of brave African and African Americans.

In the north abolitionist organizations like the Pennsylvania Abolitionist Society, a society composed mainly of Quakers, ran an organization that assisted fugitive slaves to reach Canada. Dr. Benjamin Rush, Benjamin Franklin, and Thomas Pain, were some of the non-Quaker members in the abolitionist organization, formed to do away with slavery in the United States. In the west Chief Kirjeino, of the Ottawa Indians, befriended many runaway slaves that took the U.G.R. in his direction. From Long Island's north shore Portuguese fishermen whose ancestors before them had initiated the transatlantic slave trade working side by side with the Shinnecock tribe helped escaped slaves in America to reach the free sailing ports of Massachusetts, Connecticut, and Rhode Island. John Brown grew up sharing his father, Owen Brown's, abolitionist sentiment.

"NOW, IF IT IS DEEMED NECESSARY THAT I SHOULD FORFEIT MY LIFE FOR THE FURTHERANCE OF THE END OF INJUSTICE and MINGLE MY BLOOD FURTHER WITH THE BLOOD OF MY CHILDREN AND WITH THE BLOOD OF MILLIONS IN THIS SLAVE COUNTRY WHOSE RIGHTS ARE DISREGARDED BY WICKED, CRUEL, AND UNJUST ENACTMENTS, I SAY, LET IT BE DONE."

JOHN BROWN

John Brown's house was a station on the
U.G.R. and he would spend the rest of his
adult life plotting to free the slaves in
the Union of states that had grown from
the original thirteen colonies. His
obsession would eventually cost him his
life along with the lives of a couple of
his sons.

Many southerners viewed John Brown as a
dangerous terrorist determined to upset
their way of life; a man so unbending in
his desire to destroy the institution of
slavery that he was willing to give his
life for that cause.

Carried into the crowded courtroom, still
suffering from wounds he received in his
failed raid on the U.S. armory; an action
that claimed the lives of two of his sons.
John Brown was allowed to speak to the
packed courtroom and what he had to say
troubled many of the southerners there,
when he explained how he planned to arm
the slaves and lead them in an armed
revolt against their masters leaving many
southerners to ponder such fanaticism,
perhaps even to wonder how many other
northern whites held such a conviction?
On the eve of his death, John Brown's
message was clear, the human spirit was
not meant to be chained, caged, or

prevented from developing to its full potential. That kind of injustice to someone, anywhere, should be an offense to everyone, everywhere. Thought by some to be a madman John Brown--the abolitionist showed a packed courtroom he possessed a clear head and the courage of his convictions. On December 2nd, 1859,

for his part in his failed assault at Harper's Ferry John Brown was executed. Southern slaveholders, already on edge about slave uprisings were aware of an incident that had happened a few decades before, when a tossed and blown storm damaged sailing ship eased alongside the pier in New Orleans; onboard the weather-beaten vessel were French administrators, soldiers, planters, craftsmen and their families, all survivors of the first successful slave rebellion in the western hemisphere.

The Haitian slave revolt was a complicated multi-ethnic civil war that ended with Haiti transforming itself into the first of its kind, free black republic on the island nation of Haiti.

JTHB

John Brown's involvement along with those in his mixed raiding party, made up of white abolitionist and free slaves, sent a troubling message through the south and the nation and to many his raid on Harpers Ferry showing how far some radical northern abolitionist, were willing to go to put an end to slavery. John Brown would become a martyr for the anti-slavery cause.

THE AMERICAN COLONIZATION SOCIETY

Unlike the abolitionist who saw the institution of slavery as a human rights violation and a failure of American laws to live up to the words written in the constitution, that all men were created equal. There were many white slave owners who had children by slave women. It was believed that one reason was that after the 1808 decision by the U.S. congress, to ban slaves from abroad, some owners looked at having children by a slave-woman as a way of increasing their slave headcount without the need to import or buy more slaves. A slave-woman had no say over her life, her body, nor her child's life. Slave owners who impregnated a slave woman did not want her child to grow up a slave and made arrangement through a deed of manumission, for their slave children to be free after they reached a certain age. For the slave hunter and the slave merchants, free slaves were a problem. A free slave was bad for their business, and given the lack of protection under the law, for people of color it meant some slave merchants might be put out of business themselves, so slave merchants and hunters had few reservations about turning a free man into a slave.

More than forty years before the Civil War the American Colonization Society was born.

The organization was made up of slave owners, slave merchants, and some well-meaning abolitionist. The slave owner and merchants had a vested interest in sending free slaves out of the country, and abolitionist who were convinced that African American people would never receive equal or racial justice in the United States. In 1817 when they all gathered to form the A.C.S., no slave, with or without a master, was considered a citizen of the U.S.

The purpose of the society was to set up a colony in Africa where free African Americans could be exported to live free of the discrimination they faced in the United States.

Some in the anti-slavery movement saw the American Colonization Society (the A.C.S.) for the slave holder's scheme it was, to rid the country of free African Americans.

To the proslavery plantation owners, farmers, and slave merchants, who sought to snuff out the hopes of freedom for people they saw only as property, African Americans able to purchase their own freedom or the freedom of a loved one, was bad for their business.

The process gave hope to colored people denied the opportunity to educate themselves or their children; the desire to be with their freed husband or wife was one of the main reasons so many of their spouses or children became runaways.

Despite undergoing almost constant opposition from many abolitionist groups the A.C.S organization slowly gained members along with financial support. In 1822, only five years after the organization was started the American Colonization Society was able to establish a small colony on the west coast of Africa.

The issue of Black Americans being sent to live in Africa was a problem that bothered both the slaves and some of

their white abolitionist allies. To some,
the A.C.S. goal made about as much sense
as sending white people back to England
or other native countries. Such a move
also meant that families, separated by
miles of land, would soon be separated by
hundreds of nautical miles of ocean.
After four hundred years of slavery
Africa was an alien land to many of the
colored Americans being offered the
chance to re-settle there. For most of
the refugees from discrimination, the
United States was the only homeland they
had ever known. Despite the obstacles the
American Colonization Society continued
to grow offering the promise of freedom
from terrorization, exploitation, and
segregation, along with the assurance
that slave families would be able to stay
together.

More than thirteen-thousand colored
American men, women and children were
persuaded that the west coast of Africa
could also be a promised land.
Immigration across the Atlantic Ocean to
be free of America's apartheid was
working.

American ships, financed by the A.C.S.,
would make regularly scheduled voyages to
the new colony and arrive with the tide

to deliver ship load after ship load of American colored people to the land of their ancestors. Over time the tiny American colony on the coast of Africa swelled in population and by 1847 the little settlement started by the American Colonization Society had blossomed into the independent nation of Liberia.

Confederate General Robert E. Lee freed most of his slaves shortly before the Civil War began, offering them the chance to go to the colony started by the A.C.S. in Africa at his expense. Among the slaves who chose to relocate to Liberia was the Burke family; William Burke, his wife Rosa Bella and their four children. The Burke family boarded the sailing ship Banshee, in Baltimore harbor November 1853 and along with more than 260 other immigrants sailed for the west coast of Africa. Unlike their ancestors, brought to the United States in chains four hundred years earlier, the Burkes traveled free of shackles and filled with the hope their newfound independence would bring. Behind them, in the ships' wake, Baltimore harbor faded from view as their ship made its way down the channel to the open ocean. Memories of their days in bondage, family members left behind, and their former master Robert E. Lee and his wife Mary Custis Lee went through their thoughts. The United States was the only home William and Rosa Bella had ever known. Ahead of them was an uncertain but hopeful future in a new land.

Upon their arrival in Africa the Burks would continue to communicate with the Lee family; often expressing affection for their former master. The Lee family would pass on messages to William and Rosa Bella from relatives still living in Virginia. In an 1859 edition of the publication, African Repository, some of Mary Custis Lee's letters were published. In their communications, Mary Custis Lee and Rosa Bella Burke seemed to ignore the color lines that separated the two women in the U.S., often expressing the warmth between two women who cared for each other.

Rosa Bella admitted to Mrs. Lee that colonial life in Africa was full of hardship, and that it had not been easy giving up all their immediate family connections and familiar settings in favor of the social isolation present in their unfamiliar surroundings. Aside from skin color, the Burkes had little in common with the African people or many of the slaves they had traveled there with; a situation that only seemed to compound the hardships associated with colonization in a new land.

Living as free people for the first time in their lives had given the Burkes some shelter against the hardships, in the form of a resolve that showed in Rosa Bella Burke's writings.

"I love Africa," Rosa Bella told Mary in one of her letters. "And I would not change it for America."

William Burke possessed a superior intelligence, matched only by his drive. He studied Greek and Latin at a newly established seminary in Monrovia and in 1857 he became a
Presbyterian minister. William went on to educate not only his own children, and the native children, but he would

establish many friendships by opening the door of his home to, and educating his new community, as a teacher.

These details were all chronicled in the correspondence between the Burke and the Lee family, however, news from the Burke's former home in the United States was worrisome. Unrest over the slavery issue was about to change American history forever. Political news from America only showed the growing polarization over the slavery issue was nearing a flash point. I can only assume that would have meant some stark choices for her Husband Robert E. Lee who wore a Union uniform.

It appeared that the women overall focused on keeping their communications light and cheery. Rosa Bella's news to Mary would also include the joyous news flash that she and her husband William were expecting another child. In the United States, many slaves were not allowed to name their own children. The Burkes delighted in the fact that the newest addition to their family would be born free of the unpleasant environment, about to erupt into Civil War an ocean away. More politically charged and unpleasant time would pass before the women's next communique and while Mrs. Lee's words from home indicated growing unrest between the North and South, Rosa Bella's news would bring a smile to Mrs. Lee's face. Since her last letter to the Lee's Rosa Bella had given birth to a healthy little baby girl and the smile in her words told Mrs. Lee that the Burkes were overjoyed to live in a place where their children would grow up free from the slavery they had faced in America. Life had grown much better for the Burkes since they had first arrived in Africa and in a place where she and William had the kind of freedom to name their own children, William and Rosa Bella Burke chose to name their new daughter, Martha Custis Lee Burke.

THE CIVIL WAR

Abraham Lincoln was nominated to run
for president on a platform so broad
that neither the abolitionist nor
southern pro-slavery proponents knew
for sure to which side Lincoln would
lean on the slavery issue, so basically
both sides prepared for the worst. Some
years earlier a mini version of the
Civil war had played itself out. In
1820 when the Missouri Compromise was
officially enacted, debate over whether
to make the new Missouri territory a
free state, or slave state, drove
scores of northern abolitionist and
southern pro-slavery supporters to the
newly formed territory. Each side
determined to promote their own
justifications for and against slavery.

A slave named Dred Scott who was living
in the state of Missouri sued for his
freedom on the grounds that living in a
free state made him a free man. When the
U.S. Supreme Court denied Dred Scott's
claim the court effectively overturned
all antislavery laws, by stating that,
the rights that Dred Scott was suing for
were reserved for U.S. citizens only. The
court's ruling highlighted the fact that

a slave, even if a free slave, was not considered to be a citizen of the Union of States.

It would take the passage of the 14th Amendment before African Americans were legally accepted as citizens of the United States. Missouri in effect became a pre-Civil War battleground where years of skirmishes between armed settlers from the north and south would fight it out over the slavery issue until the Missouri Compromise was repealed in 1854.

Upon news of Abraham Lincoln's election as president, Alabama, Florida, Georgia, Louisiana,
Mississippi, South Carolina, and Texas all seceded from the union, leaving North Carolina, Arkansas, Virginia, and Tennessee tittering on the brink of secession.

"THE SECESSIONIST WERE MORE THAN ZEALOUS, THEY WERE FRENZIED, DEFIANT, WRATHFUL, AND OVERBEARING. THEY INSIST THAT THE YANKEES ARE COWARDS AND WOULD NOT FIGHT; THAT IT WOULD BE A VERY SHORT WAR IN WHICH THE SOUTH WOULD ACHIEVE AN EASY VICTORY.

THE PEOPLE YIELDED TO THE STRONG CRY OF SECESSION; THE MOST STUPENDOUS BLUNDER EVER MADE BY RATIONAL MAN."

HERSCHEL V. JOHNSON

On February 4th, 1861, news of Jefferson Davis' election as president of the Confederate States of America was announced. What followed was North Carolina, Arkansas, Virginia, and Tennessee joining the other rebellious states already in secession.

President Lincoln had made it clear that he would dispatch union forces to retake any captured union forts, and that he intended to collect revenues from the rebel states.

"THIS IS A DECLARATION OF WAR AND WILL BE SO REGARDED BY THE ENTIRE SOUTH!"

HERSCHEL V. JOHNSON

The stage was set for one of the bloodiest conflicts in the United States of America since the colonial war and battle for independence with Great Britain.

A couple of months after Jefferson Davis took office the confederates went on the offensive attacking and capturing

Fort Sumter. The union flag was taken down and replaced by the confederate flag signaling the start of the Civil War.

More than a year later Abraham Lincoln would announce the following Proclamation:

THE EMANCIPATION PROCLAMATION

WHEREAS ON THE 22ND DAY OF SEPTEMBER,

A.D. 1862, A PROCLAMATION WAS ISSUED BY THE PRESIDENT OF THE UNITED STATES, CONTAINING, AMONG OTHER THINGS, THE FOLLOWING, TO WIT:

"THAT ON THE FIRST DAY OF JANUARY, A.D. 1863, ALL PERSONS HELD AS SLAVES WITHIN

ANY STATE OR DESIGNATED PART OF A STATE THE PEOPLE WHEREOF SHALL THEN BE IN

REBELLION AGAINST THE UNITED STATES, INCLUDING THE MILITARY AND NAVAL

AUTHORITY THEREOF, WILL RECOGNIZE AND MAINTAIN THE FREEDOM OF SUCH PERSON AND

WILL DO NO ACT OR ACTS TO REPRESS SUCH PERSONS, OR ANY OF THEM, IN ANY EFFORTS

THEY MAY MAKE FOR THEIR ACTUAL FREEDOM.

THAT THE EXECUTIVE WILL ON THE 1ST DAY OF JANUARY
AFORESAID, BY PROCLAMATION,
DESIGNATED THE STATES AND PARTS OF
STATES, IF ANY, IN WHICH THE PEOPLE
THEREOF, RESPECTIVELY, SHALL THEN BE IN
REBELLION AGAINST THE UNITED STATES; AND
THE FACT THAT ANY STATE OR THE PEOPLE
THEREOF SHALL ON THAT DAY BE IN GOOD
FAITH REPRESENTED IN THE CONGRESS OF THE
UNITED STATES BY MEMBERS CHOSEN THERE
TO ALL ELECTIONS WHEREIN A MAJORITY OF
THE QUALIFIED VOTERS OF SUCH STATES SHALL
HAVE PARTICIPATED SHALL, IN THE ABSENCE
OF STRONG COUNTERVAILING TESTIMONY, BE

DEEMED CONCLUSIVE EVIDENCE THAT SUCH
STATE AND THE PEOPLE THEREOF ARE NOT
THEN IN REBELLION AGAINST THE UNITED STATES."

NOW THEREFORE, I, ABRAHAM LINCOLN, PRESIDENT OF
THE UNITED STATES, BY VIRTUE OF THE POWER IN ME
VESTED AS

JTHB

*COMMANDER-IN-CHIEF OF THE ARMY AND
NAVY OF THE UNITED STATES IN TIME OF ACTUAL ARMED
REBELLION AGAINST THE*

*AUTHORITY AND GOVERNMENT OF THE UNITED
STATES, AND AS A FIT AND NECESSARY WAR
MEASURE FOR SUPPRESSING SAID REBELLION,*

DO, ON THIS 1ST DAY OF JANUARY, A.D. 1863,
*AND IN ACCORDANCE WITH MY PURPOSE SO TO DO,
PUBLICLY PROCLAIMED FOR THE FULL
PERIOD OF ONE HUNDRED DAYS FROM THE*

*FIRST DAY ABOVE MENTIONED, ORDER AND
DESIGNATE ALL THE STATES AND PARTS OF
STATES WHEREIN THE PEOPLE THEREOF,
RESPECTIVELY, ARE THIS DAY IN REBELLION
AGAINST THE UNITED STATES AND FOLLOWING, TO WIT:*

ARKANSAS, TEXAS, LOUISIANA (EXCEPT THE

*PARISHES OF ST. BERNARD, PLAQUEMINES, JEFFERSON,
ST. JOHN, ST. CHARLES, ST. JAMES, ASCENSION,
ASSUMPTION, TERREBONNE,
LAFOURCHE, ST. MARY, ST. MARTIN, AND
ORLEANS, INCLUDING THE CITY OF NEW*

ORLEANS), MISSISSIPPI, ALABAMA, FLORIDA,
GEORGIA, SOUTH CAROLINA, NORTH
CAROLINA, AND VIRGINIA, (EXCEPT THE
FORTY-EIGHT COUNTIES DESIGNATED AS WEST
VIRGINIA, AND ALSO THE COUNTIES OF
BERKLEY, ACCOMAC, NORTHAMPTON,
ELIZABETH CITY, YORK, PRINCESS ANNE, AND
NORFOLK, INCLUDING THE CITIES OF NORFOLK
AND PORTSMOUTH), AND WHICH EXCEPTED PART ARE FOR
THE PRESENT, LEFT PRECISELY AS IF THIS PROCLAMATION
WERE NOT ISSUED AND BY VIRTUE OF THE POWER AND
FOR THE

PURPOSE AFORESAID, I DO ORDER AND
DECLARE THAT ALL PERSONS HELD AS SLAVES
WITHIN SAID DESIGNATED STATES AND PART
OF STATES ARE, AND HENCEFORTH SHALL BE,
FREE; AND THAT THE EXECUTIVE GOVERNMENT OF THE
UNITED STATES, INCLUDING THE MILITARY AND NAVAL

AUTHORITIES THEREOF, WILL RECOGNIZE AND MAINTAIN
THE FREEDOM OF SAID PERSONS.

JTHB

*AND I HEREBY ENJOIN UPON THE PEOPLE SO
DECLARED TO BE FREE TO ABSTAIN FROM ALL*

*VIOLENCE, UNLESS IN NECESSARY
SELF-DEFENSE: AND I RECOMMEND TO THEM
THAT, IN ALL CASES WHEN ALLOWED, THEY LABOR
FAITHFULLY FOR REASONABLE WAGES.*

*AND FURTHER DECLARE AND MAKE KNOWN
THAT SUCH PERSONS OF SUITABLE CONDITION
WILL BE RECEIVED INTO THE ARMED SERVICE*

*OF THE UNITED STATES TO GARRISON FORTS,
POSITIONS, STATIONS, AND OTHER PLACES, AND
TO MAN VESSELS OF ALL SORTS IN SAID SERVICE.*

*AND UPON THIS ACT, SINCERELY BELIEVE TO BE
AN ACT OF JUSTICE, WARRANTED BY THE CONSTITUTION
UPON MILITARY NECESSITY; I INVOKE THE CONSIDERATE
JUDGMENT OF
MANKIND AND THE GRACIOUS FAVOR OF ALMIGHTY GOD.*

JTHB

Word of Lincoln's Emancipation Proclamation went out by telegraph, newspaper, and word of mouth. Southern slaveholders, convinced that the south would be victorious in their war against the north, denied Abraham Lincoln's message of freedom to their slaves. The rebellious southern states would choose to ignore Lincoln's Emancipation Proclamation and over the next four years thousands of men, young and old, black, and white, would be swallowed up and carried away by the fiery winds of war.

EMANCIPATION

The Civil War was still raging when Lincoln's January 1st, 1863, date went ignored by the rebel states, and even though the message of freedom held in Abraham Lincoln's Emancipation proclamation was denied to the slaves in confederate territories. Some slaves still managed to receive whispered rumors of their promised freedom circulating undercover in secret whispers, but the murmurs of freedom's approach, was still too hard for many to believe.

When a copy of Abraham Lincoln's Emancipation Proclamation was made available to Fredrick Douglas and some of his contemporaries, they carefully studied the words of the document with high hopes. Douglas had met with Lincoln on more than one occasion, at different speaking engagements, and in their conversation, Douglas was able to express to Abraham Lincoln his truest hopes and concerns about how Douglas saw slavery coming to an end.

Fredrick Douglas' concerns seem to be spread equally for both the African American people and the nation. Lincoln,

on the other hand, needed to try and control the politics that had gotten him elected. Lincoln shared nothing about his deepest personal feeling about slavery leaving the only insight into his true feeling about slavery to be picked from what he said publicly on the subject. Trying to deal with the public perception of being a Black Republican by some, Lincoln needed to show some separation between himself and the abolitionist, namely Fredrick Douglas. With the Civil War raging Lincoln's thoughts were captured in reassembling a torn nation that was split into two battling factions.
When it came to the ending of slavery in America Abraham Lincoln was about compromise. I think Lincoln had to know that his Emancipation Proclamation would not make the abolitionist happy because it was, in fact, a compromise; between openly telling the north and its union troops that they were fighting only to free the slaves or making his focus to try and repair the union. Therefore, upon closer inspection of the emancipation

proclamation document it became painfully obvious that the paper only freed the slaves in confederate held areas. The emancipation proclamation did not apply to slaves in friendly northern states. The war that few wanted, but everyone seemed to know was coming, was still being prosecuted with heavy losses on both sides.

*"WAR IS LIKE A GREAT BEAST
COMPOSED OF THE BODIES OF MEN,
WITH LITTLE RESPECT FOR LIFE, LIMB,
OR PROPERTY. ONCE UNLEASHED WAR
IS HARD TO CONTROL, IT SWALLOWS
UP MEN, WOMEN, CHILDREN, TOWNS, AND
VILLAGES, LAYING WASTE TO ALL
IN ITS PATH. WAR'S SUCCESS OR
FAILURE IS ALWAYS COUNTED IN THE
DEAD."*

Butch Gray

On one side the south fighting to dissolve the union of states and preserve a way of life that divided the nation and would forever influence America's growth.

On the other side the north fighting to preserve the union of states and reclaim the territory withdrawn by rebel forces from the union. The bloody conflict that started with Fort Sumter being bombarded into submission by triumphant rebel military, would slowly drain the southern states of its men and material.

When union forces led by General Sherman began carving a trail of death and destruction through the confederate states, some slave owners retreated further south herding their human property all the way to the last confederate refuge in the state of Texas.

After four bloody years the Civil War ended at Appomattox Courthouse with the surrender, of General Robert E. Lee's Army of Northern Virginia to union General Ulysses Simpson Grant. On April 9th, 1865, the confederate stronghold of Texas held the biggest collection of slaves anywhere in the country; more than two-hundred and fifty thousand African American women, men, and children.

Efforts to shield the slave population in the south from the words of freedom contained in the Emancipation Proclamation would be undone with the arrival of union forces. Years of speculation and rumor circulated within the slave community was laid to rest in Galveston Texas June 19th, 1865. Union Major General Gordon Granger, after assuming jurisdiction over the state of Texas, read General Order Number 3 to the gathering former slave, ex-slave owners, and captured confederate soldiers.

GENERAL ORDER NUMBER 3

"THE PEOPLE OF TEXAS ARE INFORMED THAT, IN ACCORDANCE WITH A PROCLAMATION FROM

THE EXECUTIVE OF THE UNITED STATES, ALL SLAVES ARE FREE. THIS INVOLVES AN ABSOLUTE EQUALITY OF PERSONAL RIGHTS AND

RIGHTS OF PROPERTY, BETWEEN FORMER-MASTERS AND SLAVES AND THE CONNECTION HERETOFORE EXISTING BETWEEN THEM BECOMES THAT BETWEEN EMPLOYER AND

HIRED LABOR. THE FREEDMEN ARE ADVISED TO REMAIN AT THEIR PRESENT HOMES AND

WORK FOR WAGES. THEY ARE INFORMED THAT THEY WILL NOT BE ALLOWED TO COLLECT AT

MILITARY POSTS: AND THEY WILL NOT BE SUPPORTED IN IDLENESS EITHER THERE OR

ELSEWHERE."

The announcement of General Order Number 3 to all within the sound of the General's voice made clear the enactment of the Emancipation Proclamation. A stunned slave population suddenly aware of a new way of life for themselves while at the same time, former slave owners and other slaveries supporters were left with the realization that a way of life in the south was over and gone with the wind.

After almost four hundred years, slaveries kingdom in the United States was no more. To the former slaves and their abolitionist supporters that erupted in joyous- celebration; the Emancipation Proclamation document would be elevated to the same level of importance as the Declaration of Independence for African American people.

Freedom is what the Juneteenth day celebration represents. A new beginning for thousands of African and African American people; the word slave forever replaced by the word Freemen and women.

The Juneteenth celebration evokes the memory of Abraham Lincoln's Emancipation

Proclamation, the document that was the beginning of the end for slavery in America. Slavery would be abolished as an institution in the United States December 6th, 1865, with the final ratification of the 13th Amendment.

The chance to begin putting their families back together, educating themselves, and for the first time, after the passage of the 14th and 15th Amendments, black men would be given the right to vote.

Slaves were free, but not even their abolitionist supporters seemed to know what to do next. The opposition from the anti-abolitionist would soon move back into Washington DC. Jim Crow laws would cement in place many of the prejudices held by the confederate states; prejudice that would grow into a blatant, outspoken, discrimination held in place by a carefully orchestrated system of segregation.

JTHB

"THE SLAVES HAD NOTHING BUT THEIR FREEDOM, BUT OH WHAT A GLORIOUS NOTHING IT WAS A NOTHING THAT MEANT EVERYTHING— FREEDOM!"

Butch Gray

An ending that was just the beginning is the way I like to think about it. In many ways, Juneteenth, followed by the passage of the 13th Amendment, represents not only the end of slavery in the U.S.; the celebration also represented the beginning of a new way of living and thinking for the millions of ex-slaves.

The confederate surrender ended military hostilities between the north and the south, but left smoldering the hatred mistrust and four years of fighting between the union and confederate forces had fostered.

Some confederate soldiers returning from the battlefields vowed to continue their fight against what they saw as the occupying Yankee forces from the north. The years of reconstruction that followed the Civil War would prove to be

some of the bloodiest in the nation's history for the newly freed African Americans, especially for those that chose to remain in the south. After Abraham Lincoln's assassination, southern legislators, accepted back into Washington D.C., by Vice president turned President Andrew Johnson, and who were still unhappy about the south's failed attempt to divide the union and preserve the institution of slavery, set in motion a chain of events contrary to Abraham Lincoln's desire for the end of the Civil War.

Southern lawmakers began cranking out the Black Codes; Jim Crow Laws intended to keep the black and white races apart and to institutionalize racism with "Blacks only" and "Whites only" signs.

It became illegal for African-Americans and whites to marry; share the same public parks, schools, even courthouse. For the white-owned businesses like theaters, concert halls, and stores that did not want to exclude the African American dollar, those places were divided into separate sections; one for colored people the other for whites. Much of the southern land seized by the

north and intended to be given to former slaves, under President Lincoln's plan, was returned to the confederates by vice president, Andrew Johnson.

Johnson had been chosen by Lincoln as his running mate because of his anti-slavery stand, but Johnson's reason for being against slavery was based on economics. While he disagreed with the unfair labor hold the south held by using slave labor, Johnson did not agree with Lincoln when it came to giving land once own by whites to former slaves.

"Separate but equal" was the slogan that represented the south's racist policies. Had he lived Abraham Lincoln would have been faced with the monumental task of healing the nation from four-years of bloodstained conflict to rebuilding a split union.

The Civil War had created veterans in the north and the south who were now asked to live together as one. Both sides of the divide began the long slow healing process of closing the deep national wounds between the breakaway southern states that had fought to Separate themselves from the union. For the confederate soldiers that chose not to give up and fight on, many traded their confederate uniforms for the Ku Klux Klan costume and continued the fight for their belief.

Abraham Lincoln's life was ended by John Wilks Booth, a white supremacist infuriated by the loss of his beloved southern way of life. Booth and his accomplices were tracked down, taken into custody, and executed for their crime and along with Abraham Lincoln and thousands of more became casualties of the War Between the States, the Civil War.

In the rubble of the Civil War laid the end of slavery in the southern states. For the African American people who had gone without the freedom to maintain their families, educate themselves, or earn a livable wage, the government put together a plan to extend all the freedoms they had been denied and the year 1865 would become linked with the following events:

March 3rd, 1865, after two years of resentful argument the Bureau of Refugees, Freedmen, and Abandoned Lands,

also known as the Freedmen's Bureau, was established.

April 9th, 1865, General Robert E. Lee surrendered his army to union-General Ulysses S. Grant at Appomattox Court House. General Lee's capitulation would be followed by Confederate General, Stand

Watie, surrender of his Oklahoma Cherokee fighting force, Major General Canby, General Edmund Kirby Smith, General Richard Taylor, and General Joseph Johnston, all surrendered to union forces.

April 14th, 1865, President Lincoln was assassinated, his life taken by the southern sympathizer John Wilks Booth. Lincoln's expressed goal was to preserve the union of 36 states. Before his life was taken the president had gone to the captured Confederate capital in Richmond Virginia and sat in the chair of Confederate president, Jefferson Davis. Lincoln's symbolic gesture showed that the United States constitution and the President of the U.S. held authority over all the land in the nation.

June 19th, 1865, General Gordon Grainger read General Order Number 3, delivering words of freedom to thousands of African American people in the south and opening the door for Abraham Lincoln's

Emancipation Proclamation to finally take effect and the Juneteenth Day Celebration.

June 31st, 1865, the 13th Amendment was proposed to close the loophole in President Abraham Lincoln's Emancipation Proclamation that only freed the slaves in the south. The 13th Amendment would do away with slavery throughout the entire United States.

After giving up his life at sea and his career as a slave ship captain John Newton returned to the ministry. As a child, just after the death of his mother, he was sent to a school that prepared its students for the ministry. In his youth, however, John Newton had chosen to ridicule Christianity and had been adrift from his religion for decades. To pay his bills he found work as a tide surveyor and after completing his study for the ministry he would spend the last forty-three years of his life promoting the gospel in London and Olney England. Giving thanks for what he felt was the undeserved mercy and favor from a merciful God. During his lifetime, John Newton wrote many hymns, but none were more popular than the one he titled Amazing Grace in 1770.

JTHB

AMAZING GRACE, HOW SWEET THE SOUND

THAT SAVED A WRETCH LIKE ME

I ONCE WAS LOST, BUT NOW AM FOUND

WAS BLIND, BUT NOW I SEE

TWAS GRACE THAT TAUGHT MY HEART TO FEAR AND GRACE MY FEARS RELIEVED

HOW PRECIOUS DID THAT GRACE APPEAR

THE HOUR I FIRST BELIEVED

THROUGH MANY DANGERS, TOILS AND SNARES I HAVE

ALREADY COME

TIS GRACE HATH BROUGHT ME SAFE THUS FAR

AND GRACE WILL LEAD ME HOME

Where his tombstone rest there is an
inscription on it that reads:

"JOHN NEWTON CLARK, ONCE AN INFIDEL AND

LIBERTINE, A SERVANT OF SLAVES IN AFRICA,

WAS, BY THE RICH MERCY OF OUR LORD AND

SAVIOR JESUS CHRIST PRESERVED, RESTORED,

PARDONED AND APPOINTED TO PREACH THE

FAITH HE HAD LONG LABORED TO DESTROY."

This publication was created as a
companion to the 1997 documentary I wrote
and directed, with the super long title:
"A Time to be Remembered, a Juneteenth
Story," and to share my own personal
awakening to the Juneteenth Day
Celebration. What was the first time you
ever heard of Juneteenth? If for some
reason it turns out that this written
presentation happens to be your first
realization of the Juneteenth Celebration
then you should know that the people,
places, and events mentioned here, in
connection with Juneteenth are just the
tip of the iceberg when it comes to the
history that led up to the end of slavery
in the United States.

Because of the Juneteenth connection with slavery and the fact that a lot of people, black and white, tend to focus only on the slavery issue. To me, Juneteenth celebrates the African ancestors and all they had to go through, slavery, the separation of family, no human rights, unable to vote, not considered citizens. The Civil War ended all of that for African American people with the enactment of the Emancipation Proclamation in the south.

Unfortunately, when slavery ended, racism did not. In fact, racism has continued to grow, so in effect racism has replaced slavery when it comes to the denial of equal opportunities granted to Colored Americans in the United States. Today its racism not slavery that will need the same collective abolitionist type unity and movement that eventually toppled slavery's empire.

Let me take this opportunity to update you on something I said earlier in this book because when I started writing this publication Juneteenth was not recognized as a national holiday. It is with great pleasure that I announce the Juneteenth Celebration is now a federal holiday.

A sign of the sturdy march toward equality in this nation. It took hundreds of years to do away with slavery in the United States, my hope is that it will not also take hundreds of years to do away with the racism that infects this nation.

When I first finished the companion video documentary to this handbook: A Time to Be Remembered, A Juneteenth Story it went out to colleges and Universities around the San Francisco Bay Area and when feedback started to come in from members of our test audience, one of the comments really stuck out to me. That comment was written by a woman named JoAnn Bell and said:

"How I enjoyed the viewing. All of it. History includes the bitter with the sweet and, for it to be historical it must be factual. The entire chronicle of events was done so well I wished 30 years ago I could have enjoyed this information in high school. I would have appreciated the future a little bit better and praised my ancestors a little sooner. I would have held my head a little higher and spoken a little bit louder. And like a good novel you read over and over, I hope I have the chance to view A Time to Be Remembered again and again."

This message of thanks captured pretty much the feeling I had the first time I began learning about the Juneteenth Celebration. I believe that for the American student with African ancestors there are of course plenty of depressing reasons not to remember slavery. The slave had nothing and learned to survive with the smallest of hope and the dimmest of futures.

When, in a lot of cases slavery could be endured if it meant keeping a family together. The word that Abraham Lincoln's Emancipation Proclamation would free the slaves did ignite hope in the slave community and the thought of a future without slavery was, for some, way too much to hope for. So, when Juneteenth finally arrived, and the initial shock of General Gordon Grainger's reading of General Order No. 3 did finally sink in for the former slaves, slaveholders, and slave merchants gathered in Galveston Texas the reckoning was indeed profound for everyone within earshot of the General's voice.

From there the stagecoaches, trains, and telegraph spread the word nationwide and the makings of the celebration of the end of slavery in the United States was set in motion.

Juneteenth is a part of American History because slavery is a part of American History. People who read American History books need to know and understand the meaning of Fredrick Douglass': What to the Slave is the Fourth of July to know why Juneteenth is America's true Independence Day?

Juneteenth is also a celebration of family and family gatherings, a celebration for all those African and African American souls who did not live long enough to enjoy the freedom and educational opportunities African American people enjoy today.

For more information about Juneteenth celebration ideas and Juneteenth information in general be sure to visit my Pinterest, and Website locations where you can be kept up to date about different Juneteenth events and happenings in your area.

Now let me close with some final Juneteenth notes and clarification about the Juneteenth celebration in the interest of accuracy the first official Juneteenth Celebration took place on June 19th, 1866, on the first anniversary of General Gordon Granger's reading of General Order No. 3, a year earlier in Galveston Texas.

While Juneteenth is slowly gaining the reputation for representing the end of slavery in the United States the enactment of Abraham Lincoln's Emancipation Proclamation was, at first, good news only for the slaves in confederate areas. Whether Lincoln intended to free all the slaves or not I don't know but, that is exactly what happened, all the slaves were freed, also to Lincoln's credit, he did seem to have a post war plan in place for the former slave. June 19th, 1865 was the first step in actually dismantling America's involvement in slavery and the celebration of freedom that started in the southern states after the Civil War is still spreading throughout all the rest of the states.

A Personal Note

In the years that have passed sense attending my first Juneteenth Celebration most of my family camera crew I wrote about in the beginning of this handbook have families of their own now. For those of you who might have had the chance to view my video Juneteenth presentation titled A Time to be Remembered, A Juneteenth Story, all the opening video shots of people enjoying the Juneteenth day festivities are from the part of this handbook describing my first Juneteenth Celebration experience.

Over that same time, I have developed a deep respect for the runaway slaves and the abolitionist supporters (black and white). While not all the runaways would live to see this nation turn anti-slavery their sacrifice is worth celebrating because to follow the north star to freedom, or whatever other path to freedom they chose in a hostile environment where not all black people were good, and not all white people were bad and despite some of the horrifying tortures awaiting them should they fail, to me was mind blowing.

Another important point about the end of slavery and the Juneteenth celebration is

family. It would take years and for some slaves the day would never come when they were reunited with long lost family members due to slavery. After that time African American people were able to name their own children, and for the most part keep their families together without fear of any family member being sold or taken away. So, one of the best parts of the Juneteenth Celebration to me will always be family.

The other joy I got from putting this handbook together was the feeling of finally completing my Juneteenth project started when I first put together the script for the documentary, A Time to be Remembered, a Juneteenth Story. My original script was over 200 pages long. I remember all during the planning stage for the video project being a little saddened when some part of my research included in the script had to be cut from 200 pages of script down to about 50 to 55 pages for a 58-minute video documentary.

It made finally completing the video portion of my Juneteenth project bittersweet, I was happy that part of the project was completed, and later even happier when my video project was so well received it earned me a trip to Hollywood.

I have reclaimed just about every scrap of research, quote, and character that had to be taken from my Juneteenth video and docudrama script and folded them into this companion handbook to the video so that the importance of the Juneteenth Celebration won't be lost and the hope that people will realize that Juneteenth is not only a black celebration and holiday, but an American celebration and holiday.

Unlike the July 4th, 1776, celebration, and this nations separation from the superpower of England not everyone in this nation was free, nor did everyone have equal rights under the law.

Fast forward to June 19th, 1865, the celebration of the beginning of the fall of Slavery's Empire. A collapse that would start with June 19th, 1865, and continue with the passage of the 13th, 14th, and 15th amendments and freedom and equal rights under the law, for every American, black, and white.

www.ingramcontent.com/pod-product-compliance
Lightning Source LLC
Chambersburg PA
CBHW021131020426
42331CB00005B/711